Verseweavers

the Oregon Poetry Association
Anthology of Prize-winning Poems

Number 27/2022

Oregon
Poetry
Association

Cover Design and Layout
Dale Champlin

Cover Photo Pexels; Photo by Ginny
Back Cover Photo Pexels; Forest Photograhy

Published by
Oregon Poetry Association
P.O. Box 14582
Portland, Oregon 97293-4582
oregonpoets.org

Bodycopy set in Caslon 540
Poetry set in Garamond

Printed by Kindle

First edition

10 9 8 7 6 5 4 3 2 1

ISBN 9798379009281

FOREWORD

Verseweavers was named after Oregon Poetry Association's parent organization, Verseweavers Poetry Association of Portland, founded in 1936. The competition and *Verseweavers* anthology were established in 1998 by David Hedges, then president of Oregon State Poetry Association.

We are grateful to our judges—all wonderful poets. Jessica Mehta, Beth Wood, Sherri Levine, John Witte, Susan Rich, Marc Janssen, JM Persanch, Dorothea Lasky, Michael Minassian, Amy Miller, James Benton, A. Molotkov, James R. Merrill, and Amelia Diaz Ettinger used their devotion to poetics and expertise to select the winning poems.

This year's collection covers a wide spectrum of topics and styles from traditional to experimental. Our Spring theme category was "*Ars Poetica*," the Fall theme category was "The Moon." Here you will find sonnets and golden shovels. Our outreach includes the categories of Under Thirty and Spanish Language. Our esteemed judges found the winning submissions to be *carefully crafted, engaging,* and *enjoyable*.

All poems winning cash prizes are printed on the following pages. Comments by the distinguished judges for all categories are interspersed among the winning poems. Poem titles and poets receiving honorable mention are listed after each season's winning poems.

I would like to thank contest chair Nancy Christopherson for her time and dedication to this project. OPA President, Sue Lick, and Dan Liberthson have provided invaluable expertise in proofreading this manuscript.

Complete guidelines for upcoming contests are posted on the OPA website, oregonpoets.org.

Dale Champlin, Editor

Table of Contents Spring 2022

TABLE OF CONTENTS FALL 2022

POET'S CHOICE

JUDGE Jessica Mehta

Jessica (Tyner) Mehta, PhD, and Fulbright Senior Scholar, is a multi-award-winning Aniyunwiya, Two-Spirit, queer, interdisciplinary poet and artist. As a native of the occupied land of what is often referred to today as Oregon and a citizen of the Cherokee Nation, space, place, and de-colonization are the driving forces behind her work creatively, professionally, and personally. She is currently preparing for her Fulbright Senior Scholar award and her post-doctoral fellowship as the 2022 Forecast Change Lab fellow. Jessica is currently serving as the post-graduate research representative at the Centre for Victorian Studies in Exeter, England and as a Rethink Outside fellow. Her book of experimental poems Antipodes by New Rivers Press was released in January 2022 and her picture book One of Kokum's Kids received the 2022 Lee & Low publication award. Two visual art group installations opened in January 2022 including "Strong FoundNations" at the Maddox Building in Portland as part of the GLEAN show and "Beguiled" at the Jordan Schnitzer Museum of Art. Her book We Talk of Stolen Sisters: New and Revised Poems has been chosen as a finalist for the 2022 Oregon Book Award.
Learn more at www.thischerokeerose.com.

Judge's Comments

It was an honor, and humbling, to serve as judge for this year's "Poet's Choice" category. However, it is not a position I find organic. After all, who am I to...well, you know. What we do as a "judge" is favor what we like and, as we are human/animals, that may change minute to minute. That's why I returned to all submitted poems again and again. There is skill in poetry, absolutely, but at its heart it is storytelling and as such we are drawn towards what wriggles into our core and demands to be remembered. As such, this is different for us all. As the universe would have it, three fabulous poems stood out to me, and then I was tasked with placing a number beside them. The fact that there were three—the same number I was tasked to choose—was sheer luck and I am grateful for how these stars aligned. I loved them as parents love their children: equally, but when given a Sophie's choice, I still had to choose. This does not, in actuality, make one "better" than the other, in my eyes or anyone else's (apologies of sorts to my two "Jans").

I will be honest (as poets are wont to be, at least in part)—I consider all of these winning poems "winners." That is a cliché, I know (poets are sensitive to such things). Let us remember that the desire to judge and rank is a colonial one and, as such, is always a bit feral and foreign to me. Each one made me slow down. Start digging. I saw myself in each of them. I appreciate "Dream Journal" exposing what is not and, in turn, what is. The unusual anecdotes or noticings. The dippings into fairytales before whisking me back out. I see my mother and, naturally, myself in "Pruning the Roses." I adore the word "lopping." It should be used more often, resurrected. It reminds me of Plathian language, though I cannot say for certain whether she used that term or not…regardless, lopping is exactly what we do to buds of all types. "Morning People" ushers readers across decades of a so-called "normal" life, with all its perceived ups and downs, only to bring us back to our core and remind us of the fragility and vulnerability of life and who we are. I must admit, the turtle and tortoise are sacred to Aniyunwiyas, though I am certain that was not a primary factor in my choice.

Now, as for the honorable mentions. Some readers will see that I selected only one. I was "supposed" to choose three. Let me explain. I do not think it right to (somewhat) arbitrarily choose three just because those are the lonesome, hungry number of slots. Or because of tradition. Accolades can be problematic anyway, and when I am charged with administering them I do not want to do so "just because." They should be earned and found deserving in the eyes of the one overseeing them. I asked myself if I would feel right publishing these poems as-is, either in a collection or journal. That was one of my internal bars. Excepting those I selected as winners, I found just one additional one that I would consider ready to publish: "The Fourth Generation." However, I wish there was more of it. Perhaps I want to will it into more of a form. A pantoum perhaps. It leaves me, as a reader, wanting. Still, it stuck in my brain. The haves, the have-nots, and the constant in-between we find ourselves. I would like to challenge/ask/request this writer to take it further. I do apologize to those who wished there were two more honorables, but I followed my poet-gut here. Perhaps this is a mistake, but I tried to do what was just.

I am often asked what advice I would give fellow writers, and it is simple: read great poetry. That's it. We tend to write like what we read, so read greatness—whatever that means to you. The fantastic thing about poetry is that a lot of it can be consumed no matter how busy your schedule. Pick up a collection of a favorite poet, or an anthology of best poetry of XYZ year. Read a poem a day. Skip a poem and go on to another if it turns out to be an epic and you've already stayed in bed too late and now the baby has crapped himself three times in 20 minutes and you're starting to hate yourself because you just won't be able to read a poem today. It's okay. There are much more pressing reasons to hate ourselves ("kidding" in poet). There are plenty of poems that will fit no matter what your puzzle looks like today and missing one here and there isn't going to be what kills you. Here are a few: "This is Just to Say" by William Carlos Williams. "What Women Want" by Kim Addonizio. "Lady Lazarus" by Sylvia Plath. Greatness breeds greatness. It will sink in, even if it doesn't feel like it. Be kind to yourself. Be gentle. Remember: self-love can look like poetry.

— *Jessica Mehta*

DREAM JOURNAL
Nellie Papsdorf

In this dream, I do fly.

I do not walk around my empty childhood home.

I do not suddenly know I am pregnant.

When I make eye contact on the street,
or in the pasta aisle, I am not left

wondering if it was weird that I looked so long.

I do not sit up in bed and see shadow creatures.

I save me and my brother from the wicked witch
by being nice to her and fixing her.

She was our sad old great-great-grandma all along.

In this dream, campions and ghost orchids
grow everywhere, in basements and out of the sidewalks
and they do it all the time,

always blooming, screaming in color.

In this dream, I have never filled a gas can
for a stranded stranger.

I have never learned fondness
for fluoride stains, a crowded jaw, a good gap.

NELLIE PAPSDORF is a poet and caseworker from Portland, Oregon. Her poetry has been published in *SUSAN / The Journal, HASH Journal, Witch Craft Magazine*, and *Gold Man Review*.

PRUNING THE ROSES

Lucinda Huffine

It's late February, so today I decided to prune the roses.
I got out my old shears and started lopping. Thorns grabbed me as I leaned in,
and did not let go easily.
My grandmother from Tennessee tried and failed to grow roses
in the north. She liked to talk about them, though.
To this day, when I hear "Chrysler Imperial" I don't think of a car
but of a red, red rose.
I never prune very hard, really hack them down like you're
supposed to.
In 1978 I was able to fit all my belongings in a Volkswagen Beetle.
That suited me, because I wanted to travel out west and find a new home.
That same summer my friend Kitty shaved her head because, she said,
it felt lighter and cooler that way.
Much later, I would leave a home of twenty years, and it was hard.
Being older, I was more dug in to my life. Harder
to tear loose.
So many branches broke and came down in last week's ice storm
that I imagine it will take a long while to clean them up. I lost
almost half of an old crabapple tree in my front yard.
It self-pruned itself, my neighbor said. I hope
to see it bloom in April.
To see those pink blossoms against a blue sky
and the bees humming in and out of them —-
that feels like all I need of happiness now.

LUCINDA HUFFINE is a poet living in McMinnville, Oregon.

MORNING PEOPLE

R.J. Lambert

My mother wants the sun to cool—
can it crack?—can it buckle
in the fissures of its former heat?
When my brother & I were young,
she woke us early & drove the interstate
south through desert for box turtles
whole in their shells, finding only one.
There'd been many cars. So many boxes
between apartments. Off to college,
into marriage, from divorce.
Like turtle searches, there's skill in finding
oneself at school. There's skill in getting
hitched. There's skill, also, in the keeping.
Pet books call this husbandry.
A bit paternalistic, but, at times, we could all use
a little looking after. A little after looking,
the sun like a curved palm cupped our other cheeks
returning home, an indrawn pet brought back
to wash & feed. Same time of day, now,
mom skips coffee, checks in at dawn.
Surgeons do some work in her
& alter little else. The light outweighs
her lids along the drive. Her voice still strains.
She has known two sons, but still pictures
the roadside sand, a wide blue horizon
where mountains blend into a child's face.
So long, it seems, the morning drive.
So soft under the shell.

R.J. LAMBERT (he, him, his) is an award-winning queer writer with recent poems in Denver Quarterly, New Letters, Superstition Review, and Yalobusha Review. His debut collection, Mind Lit in Neon, is newly available from Finishing Line Press. R.J. teaches writing at the Medical University of South Carolina and is online at rj-lambert.com or @SoyRJ.

MEMBERS ONLY

JUDGE   Beth Wood

BETH WOOD is an award-winning singer-songwriter and poet and believer in the power of word and song. Beth has been writing, recording, and performing for twenty-five years, and she has released twelve solo albums, one duo album, three books of poetry, and a collection of funny stories from the road. Beth's poetry book *Ladder To The Light* is the winner of the 2019 Oregon Book Awards People's Choice Award and was a finalist for the Stafford/Hall Award for Poetry. Beth's dream is to live simply, build community through music and poetry, and move something with her art. Beth's musical philosophy is that there are no wrong notes. Beth lives in Sisters, OR with her rescue dog Hannah and is continuously writing and rewriting her artist's manifesto.

JUDGE'S COMMENTS

I was honored and delighted to spend time with this collection of poems. At first it felt like a new and complete work. I read from start to finish like a book many times, marveling at the common threads running through. It was a welcome companion at my coffee table, and I treasure the time I got to spend with these carefully crafted works.

For me, a poem reaches me with maximum impact when the language is direct and succinct, when it brings to my attention something new—a new way of seeing something, or something I have not imagined yet. It brings to the surface stirred connections between the poet's experience and my own, invites me to wonder.

I humbly submit these selections, and I thank each poet for his/her/their contribution. Spending time with these poems gave me hope that poetry is alive and well in Oregon!

— Beth Wood

MEMBERS ONLY FIRST PLACE

MAKING LISTS
Jenna Funkhouser

I open a blank note on my phone,
label it "miracles."

It stays empty for a while.
I can't decide.

Sometimes I want to write, nothing.

And sometimes, everything.

It is still sitting there,
Daring me to draw a line
Down the middle of my life.

JENNA K. FUNKHOUSER is an author and nonprofit communicator living in Pacific Northwest. Her poetry has recently been published by *Geez Magazine*, *As It Ought To Be*, *Ekphrastic Review*, and the *Saint Katherine Review*, and was a runner-up in the National Federation of State Poetry Societies' Poetry Society of Indiana Award. She has imagined many lives for herself, but always ends up calling Portland, Oregon home.

MEMBERS ONLY SECOND PLACE

SANDHILL CRANES AND ELEPHANTS
Vivienne Popperl

Rows of corn stalks in flooded fields
reflect themselves. Perpendicular shadows
drop over each other, trick your eyes
so that you think "there's nothing there,"
until one grey stalk lifts up deliberately,
sets down, reveals its grey feathered
back, like a bustle, long neck, red crown.
Then you see another and another and you
hear their curling, purling, throaty call.
You learn again to be patient, to watch.

Like that time when you were ten, you sat
stifling between your brother and sister
in the back seat of the motionless car,
angled sideways to allow optimal views
of the muddy pond, and how, bored,
you looked away and then back
and a leaf swayed, then a branch,
then a herd of elephants silently sway past
brush and thorn trees, limb their way,
almost loping into brown water.

VIVIENNE POPPERL lives in Portland, Oregon. Her poems have
appeared in *Clackamas Literary Review*, *Timberline Review*, *Cirque*, *Rain
Magazine*, *About Place Journal*, and other publications. She was poetry
co-editor for the Fall 2017 edition of *VoiceCatcher*. She received both
second place and an honorable mention in the 2021 Kay Snow awards
poetry category by Willamette Writers. Her first book, *A Nest in the
Heart*, was published by The Poetry Box.

MEMBERS ONLY THIRD PLACE

SANCTUARY
Cynthia Jacobi

Just below the bump of purple vein
   she kept a hankie tucked at the top
   of her knee high nylons, left leg.
Her right hand could keep on doing
   what it needed to do –
   stir the pot or open the door
while, with the left hand, she could catch
   a sneeze, dry a tear, dab a nose.
Both arms together were sanctuary
   soft footfalls of her heart against my ear.
One Easter Sunday, she posed under naked oaks
   with her sisters, crowned
   by floral hats and sunshine
   her hankie fluttered under a polka dot hem.

CYNTHIA lives on the Central Oregon Coast. She is a visual artist
as well as a writer. After retiring as a Certified Registered Nurse
Anesthetist, she has a new focus serving her community on Newport
City Council.

NEW POETS

JUDGE   Sherri Levine

SHERRI LEVINE has published poetry in numerous journals, such as *Poet Lore*, *Clackamas River Review*, *Driftwood Press*, *Worcester Review*, *Timberline Press*, *Jewish Literary Journal*, *Mizmor Anthology*, and others. She was awarded the Lois Cranston Poetry Memorial Prize by *Calyx* in 2019. She won First Prize—Poet's Choice and second place Members Only, awarded by the Oregon Poetry Association Biannual Contest in 2017 and 2020. She published her chapbook *In These Voices* by Poetry Box in 2018. Her first full length poetry collection, *Stealing Flowers from the Neighbors*, was recently published by Kelsay Press. Sherri is the creator and host of Head for the Hills, a monthly poetry reading series and open mic. She has taught English to immigrants, refugees, and international students for over two decades. She escaped the harsh winters of upstate New York and has ever since been happily soaking in the rain. Find Sherri at www.sherrilevine.com

JUDGE'S COMMENTS

It was such an honor to read your poems. I read many of your poems while sitting in my backyard listening to the music—the Northern Flickers drumming their beaks against my chimney, the trilling songbirds in the bushes, and the squirrels scurrying across our wooden fence.

I chose "Ithaca" for several reasons. It's a beautiful well-crafted poem of place precisely detailing a long car ride both inside the car and outside during the stops. There is so much going on in this poem from the music of Willie Nelson to trespassing in a cemetery. I was moved by the last two lines where the poet states: "We balance on the barbed wire with empty beer bottles—one foot in the cemetery and the other in our backyard." Aren't we all, in a sense, doing this too? I love this poem, and I'm excited for others to read and enjoy it.

I chose "Uprooted" for its well-crafted story with such intricate details. I admire the poet's attention to detail which the poet does exceptionally well. It really drew me in, as I read it several times. The strength of this poem lies in the details of the poet's observations. Even though I found the image of the fire ants crawling through the cracked eggshell attacking the hatchling disturbing, it evoked an emotion, which for me made it a winning poem.

I chose "Dead People's Things" for the interesting details and description of the eccentric Aunt and the content of her box that the poet discovers. I love this poem because it has heart and humor. I especially laughed when I read the line written to her Aunt: "Thank you for your submission. Please try again." Ironically, this advice does not apply to this poet!

Honorary:

All three honorary mentions were enjoyable to read, some whimsical, others more profound. Truly all remarkable.

— *Sherri Levine*

NEW POETS FIRST PLACE

ITHACA
McKayla Gallup

We've been sitting for 10 hours in the state we left 10 years ago swapping
stories and the steering wheel

Letting Willie Nelson waft through the cracked window and waver over
the highway with the heat

The asphalt here has summer splits and winter warping where nothing
has been sealed since the bypass

We stop at the shell station and drink Big Red until our teeth stick to
gether when we try to talk

The gravel turns to dust while we lean against the produce sign with the
chipped beige brushstrokes blurring it

A four acre bruise of beargrass and I can't find a single stray sunflower
but rosemary still spreads from the shuttered stand

The back window by the rusting steel sink creaks when I push on the
glass but there are some places I will not crawl back to

We drive down County Road 3210 I count the cattle guards we cross and
mourn each oak tree lost to mistletoe

The creek is full now and when we walk past the No Trespassing sign I
see swallowtails settling on the granite headstones

We balance on the barbed wire with the empty beer bottles – one foot in
the cemetery and the other in our backyard

MCKAYLA GALLUP is a PNW transplant who loves everything but the
weather here. She recently started attending her local poetry group in
Vancouver, WA and began writing again.

UPROOTED
Ulrikka Haveron

She mentioned they were getting married,
that soon we'd move to his house in the sticks.
We said farewell to the familiar, transplanted
ourselves promptly to his half-finished home.

On his land, cedar trees consumed every drop of rain,
the scent of gin expelled from Juniper berries.
The rocky ground was strewn with prickly pears,
deer bones and patches of chigger-filled grass.

I transformed his unfinished bathroom into my bedroom;
Threw a thick rug on the concrete, changed the toilet
into a chair. My mother made vegan meals just for him.
He said no music, no phone calls, no showers after 8 pm.

At night, flesh toned scorpions crawled the walls,
fist-sized moths adhesed themselves to the screen door.
An orchestra of cicadas filled the thick, hot air
with their melodic song and the zip of the bug zapper.

There was no school orchestra, no French class.
My viola grew cobwebs dormant in the corner.
But there were shirtless boys in trucks by the river.
I could smoke joints with them instead of going home.

Once I found a hatching chick out on the land,
fire ants crawling into his cracked shell, stinging
him through his wet feathers before he was even born.
I picked the pissants off my new pet rooster.

In a fog of pot smoke and my headphones on,
I hovered above the sticks in a bubble of daydreams.
Young roots too tender to penetrate the rough terrain,
could shrivel or toughen on the rocky ground.

ULRIKKA HAVERON is a writer of poetry and short stories who lives in Portland, Oregon. She is originally from a family of artists in Texas. She was a performing acrobat and choreographer for 10 years and now spends her time as a lactation consultant, writer and mother. You can find her work in *VoiceCatcher* and *Star Dust Review* literary magazine.

DEAD PEOPLE'S THINGS
D. George Dreiszus

Where does it go, the fluff of life? The big chair
for sitting, numb in comfort, the books to read someday.
Affirming photos with lost meaning, papers, so important.

The box came, from hand to hand until it stopped
with me years later. "Here. I don't have room.
It was your Aunt's."

Eccentric, childless, married to a man with paper skin,
they seldom left their barren home. It was said she could have
done better. They always had a cat.

It sat dusty for months, until an idle day.
The wedding picture bright with promise, clipped obits for Mom and Pop,
several letters from home, just across the river.

Then neatly typed, in a yellow room over decades,
her poetry. And with that a note:
"Thank you for your submission. Please try again."

Buried now, the cemetery near her childhood school.
Sounds roll past from the playground of youth, the swings
alive, the bright, pure voice of immortal youth bursting like rockets.

She lives now through her words, birthed and held dear,
then set adrift through indifference to land in my soul.
Aunt Lilly, your children are home.

D. GEORGE DREISZUS attended Oregon State University, Western
Oregon University, and Babson College. He worked for many years
as a technical writer and program manager for various Oregon
technology companies.

TRADITIONAL / SHAKESPEAREAN SONNET

JUDGE   John Witte

JOHN WITTE's poems have appeared widely, in publications such as *The New Yorker, Paris Review, Kenyon Review,* and *American Poetry Review,* and have been included in *The Norton Introduction to Literature,* among several anthologies. He is the author of *Loving the Days* (Wesleyan University Press, 1978, *The Hurtling* (Orchises Press, 2005), *Second Nature* (University of Washington Press, 2008), and *Disquiet* (University of Washington Press, 2015). For thirty years he was the editor of *Northwest Review,* as well as of numerous books, including *The Collected Poems of Hazel Hall* (Oregon State University Press, 2000). The recipient of two writing fellowships from the NEA, a residency at the Provincetown Fine Arts Work Center, and numerous other grants and awards, he lives with his family in Eugene, Oregon, where he taught, until recently, at the University of Oregon. More may be found on his website: www. johnwittepoet.com.

JUDGE'S COMMENTS

The formal poem at its best pleases the ear not with its cunning but because it is organic. We can see that bilateral symmetry is the norm in nature. Consider the snowflake, or the heron, not to mention our own bodies. Thoreau opined that we should come upon a poem as we would a leaf lying on the ground, and so "read" it. And Robert Frost, the master of effortless rhyme, proposed that "the horse is happiest in harness." Accordingly, the winners in this year's category of formal verse capture this pleasing symmetry, delighting the ear without losing the ease of spoken language.

Congratulations to all the poets. And good luck with your writing.

— *John Witte*

DIAMOND CRATERS
Southeast of Burns, Oregon
Nancy Knowles

From basalt rim of lava craters, falling seems an inevitable by-blow,
akin to falling in love. We backpedal
disintegrating ash, our vertigo

just fascination with failed flight. Even
the crater itself leans over the edge,
imagines falling. And if we fell,
the crater would watch, an impassive judge,

the parent knowing this has happened before,
as crumbled boulders far below attest,
arrested mid-slide. Melted earth contorts,
subsides, in awkward ridges manifest.

But, these craters also imply older truths:
as rocks once danced, so can the falling fly.

NANCY KNOWLES teaches English and Writing at Eastern Oregon
University in La Grande, OR. She has published poetry in *Toyon*,
*Eastern Oregon Anthology, A Sense of Place, Torches n' Pitchforks, War,
Literature, & the Arts, Oregon East, Willawaw Journal, Grand Little
Things, Amethyst Review*, and *Wild Roof Journal*. She earned second
place in the Theme / The Sea category and honorable mentions in
ghazal and dizain categories from the Oregon Poetry Association.

TRADITIONAL / SHAKESPEAREAN SONNET
SECOND PLACE

Two Sides of the Window
Joy McDowell

Fourteen ways to describe the bitter cold
Folding itself around a body at work
Splitting firewood, stacking, exhausted, old,
Blazing against dense fog and winter murk.

Hands of the beloved stiff in mid-stitch
Work her coiled yarn into mittens, a cap.
Humming a tune. Fingers weave without flinch.
Snow boots stomp, glove at window, a love tap.

Fourteen ways to express adoration
With axe and crochet hook, two hearts
Labor beyond cause for calendar notation.
In home and wood, partners at precious core.

Spent youth, gained wisdom, together for more
These lovers share passage to their next shore.

JOY McDOWELL is a native Oregonian and University of Oregon
graduate. She writes from her home on Sky Mountain. Her poems
and short stories have been published nationally and internationally.

TRADITIONAL / SHAKESPEAREAN SONNET
THIRD PLACE

PEACE ROSE
Connie Soper

> *During the German occupation of France in 1940, a rose breeder near*
> *Lyon was forced to uproot his plantings for a Nazi "victory garden."*
> *He was able to smuggle out a new hybrid he had developed to the United*
> *States for safekeeping until the war ended.*

Madonna cheeks, a pearly luminance.
Lemon-chiffony skirt/ pink lipstick kiss—
a tender bloom born in war's disturbance.
Budwoods married into something new, this

bundle—sticks in burlap/soil from Lyon—
stashed in leather pouch for the attaché.
He carried it as a child of his own,
smuggled to Italy, and USA.

Fertile fields uprooted, seedlings tossed;
roses ripped from earthen beds, cedar bark.
This one survived—not forgotten nor lost;
named when Berlin fell, lifted from the dark.

Now Peace calms gazebos/gardens; sublime
haloed-scent, once slipped over enemy lines.

CONNIE SOPER is a poet and walker living and writing in Portland
and Manzanita, Oregon. Her first full length book of poetry will be
published by Airlie Press in the fall of 2022.

THEME / *ARS POETICA*

Judge Susan Rich

Seattle poet SUSAN RICH is an award-winning poet, editor and essay-ist. She is the author of *Gallery of Postcards* and *Maps: New and Select-ed Poems, Cloud Pharmacy, The Alchemist's Kitchen, Cures Include Travel* and *The Cartographer's Tongue / Poems of the World*. She has received awards from Artists Trust, PEN USA, *The Times Literary Supplement*, and the Fulbright Foundation. Her sixth book, *Blue Atlas*, is forth-coming from Red Hen Press. Her seventh, *Gallery of Postcards and Maps: New and Selected Poems*, is forthcoming from Salmon Poetry, 2022. Her work has appeared in the *New England Review*, *Image Journal*, and *Poetry Northwest* among other journals. You can visit her at www.poetsusanrich.com.

Judge's Comments

No doubt reading these strong poems during this time of COVID influenced which pieces resonated most with me. For example, today, poetry as breath includes additional meanings. Breath also recalls how the iambic foot mimics the heartbeat, how the reader's breath can hold onto silences in a poem. I must admit, I am partial to the lyric moment, to a time out of time. In "Breathing," the poet implicates herself/himself/themself: "It feels cliche asking the geese overhead/ for inspiration, so I don't," perhaps this is a nod to Mary Oliver's poem, "Wild Geese." Or perhaps the bus stop is simply under a flightpath. Either way, the poet has my attention. Yet again, in the next poem, in "Waiting," the poem is restless, it's searching for a strong location and instead finds something different than what it is searching for: "Hungry / lonely, the poem wants to go to a scenic overlook/ or maybe walk around behind the jail /where girlfriends of felons blow kisses / to the boys inside—"Here I find echoes of lines from Naomi Shihab Nye where she counsels young poets: "you might think your poem needs to go to church but really it needs to go to the dog races." And while one poem is searching out its subject-location, another poem is pursuing a reluctant poet. In different ways, these poems work to enliven the relationship between poet and subject: "green with promise. /The poem cowers in a corner /or maybe that's me."

As I read over this impressive range of poems, I keep interrogating myself as to which poems appeal to me and why. Some things are immediately apparent: concision, fresh imagery, surprising syntax. These are the nerdy poetic conventions I like to think about. And while I admit to having a certain leaning towards the surreal, this bias made me scrutinize poems with surreal elements all the more. I tried as much as is humanly possible (humanly possible for me) to put my own tastes aside and to meet each poem on its own terms. I tell my students that contained within each successful poem is a map that teaches the reader how to navigate it. May you enjoy the cartographic paths these poems offer you. Happy reading.

— *Susan Rich*

THEME / *ARS POETICA* FIRST PLACE

BREATHING
Jenna Funkhouser

I am trying, more than anything, to be
patient. No more dashing into the crush
of self-revelation. What do you want?
the silence is asking me, and I say
nothing, nothing yet. Standing at a bus
stop in the cold, simply breathing. The
sun waiting for me behind the blue haze.
It feels cliché asking the geese overhead
for inspiration, so I don't. I just watch.
Inhale. Unclench my hands.

JENNA K. FUNKHOUSER is an author and nonprofit communicator
living in Pacific Northwest. Her poetry has recently been published by
Geez Magazine, *As It Ought To Be*, *Ekphrastic Review*, and the *Saint Katherine
Review*, and was a runner-up in the National Federation
of State Poetry Societies' Poetry Society of Indiana Award. She
has imagined many lives for herself, but always ends up calling Portland,
Oregon home.

WAITING
Michael Hanner

I'm here at the bus stop waiting for a poem,
but bus after bus and no poems.
Perhaps they took the train and are now
idling around the station waiting for a poet
to stop and give them a lift,
find a stub of a pencil,
an old ball point,
a sheet of cold white paper
empty as the moon. Hungry, lonely,
the poem wants to go to a scenic overlook
or maybe walk around behind the jail
where girlfriends of felons blow kisses
to the boys inside–
listen for their low moan
as they crush out their smokes,
look back up at the faces
in the small bright windows.

MICHAEL HANNER is an architect whose poems are found in *Spillway*, *Timberline Review*, *Shark Reef Review*, *Nimrod*, *Cloudbank*, *Rhino*, *Southern Humanities Review*, *Gargoyle*, *Mudfish* and others. His most recent books are *Alice*, 2021, *More Alice*, 2021, *Adriatica*, 2016 and a guide book, *Le Bugue, Black Périgord & Beyond*, 2016. He loves Toni Hanner, sharp scissors, Esterbrook pens, travel, irony, English croquet, French cooking and Argentine tango.

I Try and Run Away from the Poem, an *Ars Poetica*
Donna Prinzmetal

But I keep coming back.
The hunger for syllables
unravels me.
Once I was lost in a spiral geography,
maps I couldn't follow.
The wind was whistling so hard
I could barely hear the poem
mumbling from the deep inside of things,
winding through me like smoke.
This poem is keeping a secret.
Dust speckles a shaft of sun through a window.
A door opens to a narrow dream,
green with promise.
The poem cowers in a corner
or maybe that's me.
You know what it's like to hear bones chatter,
their ghostly clicks and whispers.
That's what this poem is doing now,
letting me know what I know
which is absolutely nothing.

DONNA PRINZMETAL is a poet, psychotherapist and teacher. She has taught poetry and creative writing for more than 30 years to adults and children. Her poems have appeared in many magazines, including *Prairie Schooner*, *The Comstock Review*, *The Journal* and *Verseweavers*. Her first book, *Snow White When No One Was Looking*, was published with CW Books in May of 2014. She is the recent recipient of the 2020 Lois Cranston Prize from *Calyx Journal*.

30 AND UNDER

JUDGE Marc Janssen

MARC JANSSEN has been writing poems since around 1980. Some people would say that was a long time but not a dinosaur. Early decrepitude has not slowed him down much; his verse can be found scattered around the world in places like *Pinyon*, *Slant*, *Cirque Journal*, *Off the Coast*, *Poetry Salzburg*, and in his book *November Reconsidered*. Janssen coordinates the Salem Poetry Project—a weekly reading, and the occasionally occurring Salem Poetry Festival, and was a nominee for Oregon Poet Laureate. For more information visit, marcjanssenpoet.com.

.

JUDGE'S COMMENTS

When I read poetry I look for language that surprises and engages. It seems cliché to say it that way. What does that even mean? Sometimes poems grab you, they live with you for a while, even if you don't want them to. After all, it is just words, but if put in the right order, they sit on paper like bear traps waiting for someone to step on them. All the three of the 30 and Under catagory had that element in them.

"Belshazzar" draws on two stories. One is the character the poem is named for, Belshazzaar, the Babylonian king who is a tyrant who elevates Daniel to a high office. The second is Tantalus, who was punished by being in a place with food and drink he could not access. There is tension in this poem that invites deep reading.

The twist at the end of "Elmer" is worth the wait. I enjoyed being led one way then spun around in another direction.

— *Marc Janssen*

30 AND UNDER FIRST PLACE

BELSHAZZAR
McKayla Gallup

This is my father's table but he stands at the foot
Toasts to power and prayer echo off empty bowls
Mix with the incense and steam and then the screams
When my skeleton is scraped from the cauldron
He'll still call this a curse while he waits for the water to rise
Claws for the apple and tells the gods they always asked for everything
If there is mercy in this myth it is not for Tantalus
I am sacrifice and sacrilege and still simmering

I am not my father but I will sit at his table
Crush the glass with the grapes under my heel
Mull the blood with the wine and let it pool past my teeth
Spill from my tongue to yours until I lose my reflection
Search for it in the shards I cough up into your waiting palms
What warning are words on the wall when they are written under wallpaper
If there is a hand in this haunting it is not holy
We are wicked and weighed and found wanting

I will set my table with salt and silver
Save a place for every soul that seeps through
The cracks and caution tape and caulked windows
And when I find myself coming home by crossroads
Drop the rotting thing in my mouth on the welcome mat
Gut the kitchen and peel back the floorboards until my bones are bared
If there is a spirit in this summoning it is safe now
This is feast and faith and the full moon waning

McKAYLA GALLUP is a PNW transplant who loves everything but the
weather here. She recently started attending her local poetry group in
Vancouver, WA and began writing again.

30 AND UNDER SECOND PLACE

ELMER
Christopher Foufos

I have never seen anyone
confront Father Time with such humility.
After a life of abuse and toil
he braved his twilight with quiet defiance.
Season upon season he endured the elements,
never betraying his post.
He was a sentinel, modest and vigilant;
with a solemnity to his station.
Despite a body and spirit of such sturdy composition,
he too began to decay.
His encroaching departure highlighted the dualities attached to life:

For one to grow it must also wither.
Motion cannot exist in the absence of stillness.
Life carries its intrinsic value, for it is accompanied by death.

The color and vibrancy of his flesh
paled as he navigated his inevitable denouement.
He fell to permanent silence
in a field by the barn.
The golden autumn grass
accentuated his fading blue.
Some called him an old pickup truck;
a disservice to his loyalty.
A 1971 Dodge.
We called him Elmer.

CHRISTOPHER FOUFOS was born and raised in the small rural town
of Dundee, Oregon. He is 26 years old with an undergraduate degree
in Social Science with an emphasis on Anthropology and Indigenous
Studies. His passions lie in writing and travel, so he wishes to
eventually graduate from his oh so romantic position of moving
boxes in a warehouse to a career in which he can pursue something
in those fields. He ultimately allows the fluidity and unpredictability
of life to dictate where he goes and what he is doing, so for now he
is content with that process.

30 AND UNDER THIRD PLACE

TOUGH COOKIE
Nellie Papsdorf

The dream is dead. Long live the dream.

Into gestalt. Into shortcuts. That tasty moment
where you remember you can look up at the sky.

Isn't it funny how I forget how good
a good tangerine tastes?

How I can remember?

I will never get this
quite right. I spill everywhere.

So thank dog
for long cons, functional resumes,
pass/fail grades.

The sun for now keeps coming. I keep on
occasion marveling at lone beetles, snowdrops,
a cloudy natural ubiquity.

If it weren't for all this world,
I wouldn't.

The dream is over. Long live the dream.

NELLIE PAPSDORF is a poet and caseworker from Portland, Oregon.
Her poetry has been published in *SUSAN / The Journal, HASH
Journal, Witch Craft Magazine*, and *Gold Man Review*.

SPANISH LANGUAGE

JUDGE   JM Persanch

JM PERSANCH is a poet and author of fiction. He was awarded
first prize in the I Contest of Poetry in Andaluz, directed the
literary group *Palabras Indiscretas* for five years leading to the
publication of five collections of poems, and has extensively
published in several magazines in Europe, Latin America and
the US, including the anthologies *Moments Before Midnight*
and *Terra Incognita* in Oregon. He often participates in public
readings including the Salem Poetry Project. JM Persanch is a
writer who appreciates creative forms as a path to both exploring
human nature and better understanding contemporary societies.
For further details as well as for a comprehensive list of projects and
publications, see his personal webpage: https://jmpersanch.com.

JUDGE'S COMMENTS

MI DOBLE VOZ by Nitza Hernandez
  The poem speaks to your heart, soul, and mind, reuniting,
healing a broken self. It imbues the reader in an old trope with a
renewed spirit, drawing parallels with Anzaldúa's "wild tongue"
fused with the epic of Corky González. As a result, life and history
merge naturally while embellished by a sensible selection of words
as well as by a great sense of cadence which resembles that of
a passionate lullaby.

CANTO DEL NÁUFRAGO by German Rizo
  The poem catches the reader in a spider web infused in a
nihilistic thread of in crescendo metaphors, making it theatrical,
making it real, as truthful as life and death themselves. It reminds
us of the futile, disoriented contemporary self, to perhaps allow a
glimpse into an awakened consciousness.

HÉROES ESENCIALES by Raul Sanchez
  The poem allows a glimpse of the invisible, as it is worthy of
keeping memories alive. Written with everyday prose, the poem
parallels the language of those it portrays, providing voices to the
often voiceless.

— JM Persanch

MI DOBLE VOZ

Nitza Hernandez

1

Escribo poesía en dos lenguas / dos idiomas
mis sentimientos en español son transparentes
los acentos y las Ñs corren libres por mis venas,
mis pensamientos en inglés a veces fluyen
como cintas que giran a lo largo de una página rota.

2

Mi lengua materna / Ñ / no vive dentro de mi boca,
más bien respira en medio de mis entrañas
adherida a mi alma reencarnada
desde tiempos y espacios ancestrales.

La piel de tambores africanos convoca mis caderas
viejas memorias   de bomba y bongó,
danza de negras esclavas   con su dolor.

Lágrimas de sangre resuenan con espanto,
maracas y cantos de guasábara gritan en el yucayeque
como lenguas de aguas turbulentas lamiendo el borde de las costas
para enfrentar el genocidio / Agueybaná a la vanguardia
guerreras taínas perspicaces / Anacaona, la Flor de Oro, en mando
el amor de Yuisa la cacica   por un mulato,
intento fallido de forjar puentes.

¡Perdono a la historia por difamar corazones libres!

3

Mi lengua materna / Ñ / es testigo de los crujientes pisos rotos
de osadas carabelas   en largas travesías por el Atlántico,
es testigo de sueños enardecidos por la conquista de nuevas tierras.
En mi lengua   también hay huellas de taconeo
de pioneras españolas   aventureras
su pasión vibrante tocando al ritmo de guitarras y castañuelas.

Así pues, mi español es una hermosa amalgama de existencias sonoras
una lengua ondulada de tierra   en medio del mar
un archipiélago labrado con mil tonos de colores y voces.

4

El inglés / EN / tampoco vive dentro de mi boca
más bien viaja curioso   por los bordes de mi espíritu
con ambiguas memorias de tiempos diferentes de conquista
segunda ronda colonial en el Caribe / encubierta / tras bastidores.

5

Al fin y al cabo / la esencia de mi lengua es   una doble voz
de múltiples idas y regresos / un intenso aleteo de mi corazón abierto
como colibrí   en vuelo libre   anunciando un nuevo amanecer
haciendo poesía más allá del tiempo / en dos idiomas,
una voz de tierra y sabiduría derramada en los ríos profundos de mi alma.

SPANISH LANGUAGE FIRST PLACE

ENTRE PARÉNTESIS   (ENGLISH TRANSLATION)
Nitza Hernández

1

I write poetry in two tongues / two languages
my feelings in Spanish are transparent
accents and Ñs run free through my veins
at times my thoughts in English flow
like ribbons spinning along a broken page.

2

My mother tongue / Ñ / does not live inside my mouth,
it rather breathes in the middle of my entrails
attached to my reincarnated soul
from ancient times and spaces.

The skin of African drums summons my hips
old memories   of bomba and bongó
dance of enslaved black women   with their pain.

Tears of blood resound with horror,
maracas and guasábara songs scream in the yucayeque
like tongues of rough waters lapping the edge of the shores
to confront the genocide / Agueybaná at the vanguard
keen Taino women warriors / Anacaona, the Golden Flower, in command
the love of cacica Yuisa   for a mulatto
a failed attempt to build bridges.

I forgive history for defaming free hearts!

3

My mother tongue / Ñ / is a witness of the creaking broken floors
of daring caravels   on long journeys across the Atlantic,
is a witness of burning dreams for the conquest of new lands.
In my tongue   there are also traces of the heel tapping

of Spanish pioneer women   adventurous
their vibrant passion playing to the rhythm of castanets and guitars.

Thus, my Spanish is a beautiful blend of sonorous existences
a curling tongue of land   in the middle of the sea
an archipelago carved with a thousand shades of colors and voices.

4

English / ENG / too does not live inside my mouth
instead it travels curiously   along the edges of my spirit
with ambiguous memories of different times of conquest
a second colonial round in the Caribbean
undercover / behind the scenes.

5

But in the end / the essence of my tongue is a two-fold voice
of multiple departures and returns / an intense flutter of my open heart
like a hummingbird in free flight   announcing a new dawn
making poetry beyond time / in two languages,
a double tongue of land and wisdom spilled into the deep rivers of my soul.

NITZA M. HERNÁNDEZ LÓPEZ (aka NITZA HERNANDEZ) is a Puerto Rican
poet, visual artist/and photographer living in Salem, OR since 2012. Her
poems have appeared in /pān \dé \mïk /2020: An Anthology of Pandemic
Poems, Terra Incognita (Bob Hill P), Antologías de Poesía Oregoniana, and
lalibreta.online, among other anthologies. She has won poetry awards
from the Oregon Poetry Association and the Instituto de Cultura
Oregoriana. She often reads her poems at the Salem Poetry Project.

Canto del náufrago I
German Rizo

Sin otro dolor que el de sucumbir
frente a ese ruido extraviado
llevando la costumbre
de un animal a tientas.

Quiero salir de ese subyugado cuerpo
ofrecer los escombros a la libertad /
despoblar este destierro fatídico
sin ecos / ni raíces en agonía /
consagrado en la demencia
para no ser el eje de un moribundo
ni volver a ese abismo cercado
en la memoria.

Seguir la entreabierta hendidura
por donde un sollozo gotea
el final de un augurio.

Seguir la sentencia aprisionando
las muecas destinadas a curar el vacío
conteniendo los ardores de la sangre.

Canto del náufrago II

No tengo ideas / no hay espacios
aquí flota la sed
y la lluvia desangra su dolor.

Hay multitud de estallidos
es tarde y me enredo
en el vuelo de los pájaros.

Beso lo siniestro de la niebla.
Ella danza en lo misterioso del Edén
sus manos recogen
las espinas de mi rostro.

No tengo huellas
ninguna sombra
acompaña mi corazón.

Me arrastran los alaridos de un lobo
y tengo miedo.
Los huesos envenenan mi sangre
y me devora la manía del reloj
acosando las paredes.

No hay nadie
y el polvo en el corazón
es un collar de ecos.

Tejo en la pared
la hora de la muerte.

SPANISH LANGUAGE SECOND PLACE

CASTAWAY CHANT I   (ENGLISH TRANSLATION)
German Rizo

With no other pain than surrendering
before the forlorn clatter
sporting the practice
of a groping animal.

I want to exit that subjugated body
offer the rubble to freedom /
clear out this fateful exile
no echoes / no roots in agony /
enshrined in dementia
so as not to be the axis of a dying man
nor return to the memory of
that fenced abyss

To keep to the half-open cleft
where a howl trickles
the end of a prophecy.
To keep to the sentence imprisoning
the grimaces destined to heal the emptiness
holding the passions of the blood.

CASTAWAY CHANT II

I have no notions / there are no spaces
thirst floats here
and the rain bleeds her pain.

There are many bursts
it's late and I become entangle
in the flight of birds' flight.

I kiss the sinister side of the mist.
She dances in the mystery of Eden
his hands pick up
the thorns on my face.

I have no footprints
nor a single shadow
shepherds my heart.

The howls of a wolf drag me
and I'm fearful.
The bones poison my blood
and the clock-mania devours me
pestering the walls.

There is no one
and the dust in the heart
is a necklace of echoes.

I weave on the wall
the hour of death.

GERMÁN RIZO is a Mexican poet and narrator. He published: *Un pájaro ciego sale de mi boca* (2022), *Cantos del alma y la vida* (2014), *Bajo la sombra del corazón* (2016, *Atráeme contigo* (2017), and *Huellas tras lluvia* (2020). His work has appeared in the following anthologies: *Equilibrios contrarios, tributo a Federico Garcia Lorca* (2015); *Anthology of Oregonian Poetry* (2018) in Portland, Oregon; *The Other Voice* (20); and in the anthology *Flores by Youtan Poluo* (2021). He won Second Prize for poetry at the V María Eloísa García Lorca International Competition with his poem "Vendra la noche," carried out by the National Union of Writers of Spain (UNEE, 2017). He also won third place in the first edition of the literary contest LETRA D' KMBIO, with "Que sangren mis manos," in Havana Cuba. (2017).

SPANISH LANGUAGE THIRD PLACE

HÉROES ESENCIAALES
Raúl Sánchez

Y un día el mundo se convirtió en una placa de Petri...
La tos de alguien pudo ser una sentencia de muerte.
El aire envenenado, aire vivo, aire peligroso.
Asustados; escuchamos, obedecimos,
nos lavamos las manos; constantemente...
Sonreímos detrás de las máscaras,
distanciados, vivimos en nuestros capullos.
Detrás de puertas y ventanas cerradas.

Nos apartamos de toda persona a menos de dos metros de distancia.
Llenos de pánico recogimos el correo, sacamos la basura.
Escuchamos, nos preocupamos, mientras que otros no lo hicieron.
Algunos de nosotros sobrevivimos, aun así, no pudimos salir.
¡Mágicamente se descubrió una red oculta!
Los trabajadores anónimos e independientes se convirtieron:
¡En esenciales y sin licencia!
¡Un nuevo grupo de héroes, el nacimiento de una nueva generación!

¡El trabajador ordinario se convirtió en un HÉROE!
Una parte esencial de la sociedad.
La misma sociedad que los ve como gente ordinaria,
o indocumentada y sin experiencia.
Sin embargo, se volvieron esenciales para todos.
Trabajaron no solo porque necesitaban dinero,
sino porque pudieron hacerlo.
Arriesgando sus propias vidas por todos los demás.

Entregaron comida, cuidaron de nuestros ancianos y discapacitados.
Entregaron paquetes, surtieron los estantes,
hicieron mandados, cambiaron sábanas en los hospitales.

Sus salarios bajos no les impidió trabajar.
Trabajadores esenciales, una designación otorgada
a todos los que lucharon contra el virus.
Superaron sus luchas y miedos y, sin embargo,
algunos de ellos no sobrevivieron.

Los privilegiados experimentaron una cruda "realidad".
Además de la comida, también hicieron compras pandémicas,
frívolas en el mejor sentido de la palabra para aliviar sus mentes ansiosas.

El trabajador esencial se convirtió en una persona digna
que perdurará como un apodo… representando la unidad,
el sacrificio, la participación, interconexión
y atención sin prejuicios
para todos los americanos.

ESSENTIAL HEROES   (ENGLISH TRANSLATION)
Raúl Sánchez

And one day the world became a petri dish—
Someone's cough could be a death sentence.
Poisoned air, living air, dangerous air.
Scared; we listened, we followed,
we washed our hands, constantly—
We wore our smile behind the masks,
distanced, we lived in our cocoons.
Behind closed doors, windows shut.

Avoided everyone and anyone within six feet.
Panicked to get the mail, to put out the trash.
We listened, we cared, while others did not.
Some of us survived, yet we could not go outside.
Magically a hidden network was discovered!
Unnamed and independent workers became:
Essential, without a license!
A new brand of heroes, a new generation born.

The ordinary worker became a HERO!
An essential part of society.
The same society that sees them as ordinary
or undocumented and unskilled.
Yet, they became essential to all.
They worked not only because they needed money,
but because they could.
Risking their own lives for everyone else.

They delivered food, took care of elders and the disabled
delivered packages, stocked shelves,
ran errands, changed sheets in hospitals.

Their low wages didn't keep them from working.
Essential workers, a name given to all who fought
against the virus.
They overcame their struggles and fears and yet,
some of them didn't survive.

The well to do experienced a crude "reality".
Besides food, they made Pandemic purchases,
frivolous at best to alleviate their anxious minds.
The essential worker became the banner word
that will endure as a moniker
representing unity, sacrifice, involvement,
interconnection and care without prejudice
for all Americans.

RAÚL SÁNCHEZ is WA Poet Laureate for the for City of Redmond. He teaches poetry in Spanish through the WITS and Jack Straw Cultural programs. He volunteered for PONGO Teen Writing at the Juvenile Detention Center. His second collection *When There Were No Borders* was released by Flower Song Books, McAllen Texas July 2021.

SPANISH LANGUAGE HONORABLE MENTIONS

LECCIONES DEL RÍO by Broderick Eaton

The poem connects to a long Spanish tradition of the symbolism of water, and particularly rivers, dated back to Jorge Marique's Coplas a la Muerte de su padre in the fifteenth century. It however offers a vitalist outlook, allowing life to naturally flow through the readers' eyes, who also embarks to reflect, learn the lessons from their own river.

ALABANZA A LO QUE AGRADEZCO by Amelia Diaz Ettinger

The poem attempts to bridge between memories, making the art of poetry worthy as a tool for self-reflection, while offering nature a central stage and forcing the reader into the oxymoron of voiced silences as part of the process of listening.

UN RÍO DE SANGRE by Efrain Diaz-Horna

Poetry is many things, one of them can also encompass—as the poem evidences—a form of self- exploration seeking identity as well as working through to come to personal terms with history to find peace of mind.

Thank you, I have enjoyed serving as a judge. It has always been fascinating to me how poetry survives through the ages cultivating the noble art of shedding light and comfort to those in need. The process somehow reconnected me with my past self, bringing it to my presence to share a few thoughts and memories… I´ll perhaps need to write a note, or poem, to 'future me.'

Every poet, every poem is—in a sense—unique; know yourself first. Publishing and being known by others are the anecdote, knowing yourself is the prize.

—*JM Persanch*

SPRING 2022 HONORABLE MENTIONS

POET'S CHOICE
HONORABLE MENTION: "THE FOURTH GENERATION"
   by Gigi Cooper

MEMBERS ONLY
1ST HONORABLE MENTION: "MR. POLICEMAN"
   by Scottie Sterrett
2ND HONORABLE MENTION: "COMMUNION"
   by Nancy Knowles
3RD HONORABLE MENTION: "VALOR AND OBEDIENCE"
   by Susan Whitney

NEW POETS
1ST HONORABLE MENTION: "THE TETONS"
   by Christopher Foufos
2ND HONORABLE MENTION: "FOR JACQUES"
   by Marianne Bickett
3RD HONORABLE MENTION: "PINK"
   by Rin Ehlers Sheldon

TRADITIONAL / SHAKESPEAREAN SONNET
1ST HONORABLE MENTION: "THE RACE"
   by John McPherson
2ND HONORABLE MENTION: "MISTRESS LUCE'S SOLILOQUY:
   SHAKESPEARE'S SONNET 130, PLAN B"
   by Susan Woods Morse
3RD HONORABLE MENTION: "FINDING LOVE ONLINE"
   by David Hedges

THEME / *ARS POETICA*

1st Honorable Mention: "Nothing Up My Sleeve"
    by Nancy Knowles
2nd Honorable Mention: "Lunch with the Surrealists"
    by Carey Taylor
3rd Honorable Mention: "Toolbelt"
    by Dan Kaufman

UNDER 30

Honorable Mention: "This is Definitely Not a Metaphor"
    by Brady Pearson

SPANISH LANGUAGE

1st Honorable Mention: "Lecciones del río"
    by Broderick Eaton
2nd Honorable Mention: "Alabanza a lo que Agradezco"
    by Amelia Diaz Ettinger
3rd Honorable Mention: "Un rio de sangre"
    by Efrain Diaz-Horna

POET'S CHOICE

JUDGE Dorothea Lasky

DOROTHEA LASKY is the author of five full-length collections of poetry and one book of prose, the newest of which is Animal (Wave Books). Her work has appeared in *POETRY*, *The New Yorker*, *The Paris Review*, *The Atlantic*, and *Boston Review*. She holds an MFA from the University of Massachusetts-Amherst and a doctorate in creativity and education from the University of Pennsylvania. She also studied at Harvard University and at Washington University. She has taught poetry at NYU, Wesleyan University, and Bennington College. In 2013 she was a Bagley Wright Fellow in Poetry. Currently she is an Associate Professor of Poetry at Columbia University's School of the Arts, where she directs the Poetry concentration in the MFA program, acts as a co-faculty advisor for Columbia Artist/Teachers (CA/T), and organizes the summer writing program. She lives in New York City. Visit her at https://www.dorothealasky.com. Twitter and Instagram: @dorothealasky

La Chua

Alison Gaines

This is the only place
I was ever happy, you said,
describing the place down the road
where leathery reptiles emerge
from dark, shallow water;
where fast-growing hyacinths
support the weight
of the neon-iridescent birds
that hurry, yellow-legged, across them,
where small raptors circle for snails,
coming back around
like clockwork.
The screech of other invasives
fills the air and the slight
stink of the swamp rises,
and it pleases you.
Why is this place happiness?
Where else is everything so
laid bare, limitless,
not concealed
behind thick stands of trees
or rocky foothills?
Here, families of a dozen
small chicks paddle out
amidst what may kill them.
Sadness does not conceal itself here,
and what's hiding must be flushed out
from the clumps of reeds
to face the sun, or the heavy gray clouds,
or whatever is reflected
past where the boardwalk
will take you.

ALISON GAINES lives in Portland, Oregon where she teaches high school English. She holds a BA from Knox College and an MFA in poetry from the University of Florida. Her work appears in several journals including *Salamander* and *The Southern Review*.

AT ST. MARY'S

SUZY HARRIS

   —after Lucille Clifton's "blessing the boats"

when all is said and done, may
we recognize how the tide

brings us back to all that
we ever knew, all that is
forever inside us, entering
and leaving, stroking and breathing, even
when we least know it, now

and before, how the lip
of the wave rolls over grains of
sand. no one knows our
story, even those with understanding.

still, we try. here, let me carry
your bag for a moment while you
walk beside, our bare feet making tracks out

of the small village, beyond
the cafes that line the beach to the face
of the rock at the headlands, where we let go of fear

and find our way back down again. may
we remember this sky, this sun. May you
face your loss with a kiss,

the strength of the wind,
resolve of the ancestors, then
when you are ready, turn
away from it all, from
the past with its smallness, and find it

a new home, maybe a carved box, a certain

place that will appreciate all that
it was meant to be. perhaps it
will free you to find a new way, will

leave you changed. love
will find its way back into your
hands, your breath, back
into whatever may
come next for you

now count to ten and open
your heart. Listen to your
fears, close your eyes
and remember how to
swim under water

that feeling of gliding under water
breathless and waving
with the water's motion forever

breast-stroking through long glides and
surging back into your own body. may
your loss not define you
and when you are ready in
that moment your
grace and innocence

will sail
home again through
what is no longer the empty place, this
place of sun and sand, to
the unknown but welcoming that

SUZY HARRIS has recently served as poetry editor of *Timberline Review*. Her chapbook *Listening in the Dark*, about losing her hearing and learning to hear again with cochlear implants, was published by The Poetry Box in February 2023.

Pink Bubble Technology™
DM Wallace

Anyone can put a pink bubble around themselves,
and once you know how to do it you will wonder
how you ever got through life without it!

Your pink bubble looks exactly the way you
think a pink bubble should: glossy, soft and round,
flowing, opalescent and clear, you get the idea.

Put yourself right inside your pink bubble
and look around, letting it expand and change
as you take in all of its aspects of light and shape.

Now float around in there feeling the sweet
comfort and ease of being surrounded by
this ever encompassing and perfect embrace.

The pink bubble will be your friend and ally
in many situations where you need absolute clarity:
walking, speaking, driving, and especially listening!

Get to know your pink bubble intimately,
visualizing exactly how it feels and functions
and calling it to yourself whenever you want.

Your tasks will get done effortlessly. People will
open their hearts to you and appreciate your ideas,
all physical and energetic obstructions evaporating.

People around you might notice something different
about you, and you will begin to see shifts in time and
space occur as you fully engage with this technology.

DM WALLACE grew up in a large Catholic family in Twin Falls, Idaho, but she has lived in Eugene, Oregon for over 40 years. She has been published in numerous literary journals and one anthology. Her book Lexicon of the Body was released from Atmosphere Press in 2022. She has worked as a poetry editor, a film reviewer, an event coordinator and wine sales rep, and is a new member of OPA.

POET'S CHOICE HONORABLE MENTIONS

JUDGE'S COMMENT

In addition to the winning poems I also enjoyed, in no particular order:

SNAPSHOT: THE COW & THE GIRL by Louhi Pojola
BIRD HOUSE by Kari Hakan
THE END OF SOMETHING by Vivienne Popperl
COMFORT FOUND IN A BOX OF CREAM OF WHEAT
    by Shawn Aveningo Sanders

— *Dorothea Lasky*

MEMBERS ONLY

JUDGE   Michael Minassian

MICHAEL MINASSIAN is a contributing editor for *Verse-Virtual*, an online poetry journal. His poetry collections *Time is Not a River*, *Morning Calm*, and *A Matter of Timing* are all available on Amazon. A new chapbook, *Jack Pays a Visit*, was released in 2022. For more information: https://michaelminassian.com

JUDGE'S COMMENTS

FIRST PLACE—BREAKING: This is an exceptional poem. The setting is vividly described and the poet uses imagery in fresh and exciting ways "the parched earth forgets how to swallow"—a terrific image on its own, but coupled with the wilting flowers in the next line, sets up the reader for the turn that comes so powerfully in the latter part of the poem. The poet takes us in a direction we don't expect: "Somewhere in Florida, cancer has arrived like a hurricane in my aunt's body." The ending is another subtle shift, bringing a universal turn to what seems to be a very personal poem.

SECOND PLACE—STILL LIFE: This poem describes the painter, the subject of the poem, sketching in details in a concise and economical way. The painter, perhaps past his prime, still has other possibilities open, some revisited from his youth, weaving in rich details. These striking lines give the reader a vivid portrait, "He might learn to use Twitter/or get high and play every one of his Dylan albums/in chronological order, listening to Blonde on Blonde twice." The poet uses examples from nature to suggest the passage of time and the aging process, rounding out the process. The closing lines in the poem leave the reader with a final image, unexpected and sharply observed. A poem worth returning to more than once.

THIRD PLACE—AUDACIOUS: This poem is a delight to read, surprising the reader along with the speaker of the poem as she recounts her friend's shocking and revealing words. Told in a conversational tone, we get insights into the friend's personality as well as the speaker who is mildly shocked, curious, and perhaps a little bit jealous. It's a poem that will have you smiling and nodding in recognition of human behavior.

— Michael Minassian

BREAKING
Jennifer Rood

JENNIFER ROOD has taught English, art, and social studies in Southern Oregon for the past 30 years. She has been previously published in *Verseweavers*, as well as in other journals and anthologies. She served on the OPA Board from 2018 – 2021, including a year as President.

The day is hazy, hot, and still. Thunderclouds bloom in the far distance behind dark mountain silhouettes. I go out to water, but days like this, the parched earth forgets how to swallow, and water just runs along the ground looking for a hiding place. Flowers wilt by afternoon, and I have to let them because I don't know the spell to say to break the heat. They say rain is coming, but I can't feel it yet, and right now it's about as useless as hope, anyway. Somewhere in Florida, cancer has arrived like a hurricane in my aunt's body. She is dying, and there's another spell I do not know: I don't know how to break disease from her. I don't think a prayer works the same as a spell does, although I have wished it would. It's all I can do, though. So I say a prayer of breaking. For her. For us all.

STILL LIFE
Linda Drach

Of all the paintings he made in his life,
the round-bottomed pears, the Chinese lantern pods
artfully crouched around bottles of wine,
only a few remain, and the studio has grown dusty.
He could go in there if he wanted, pick up
a brush with arthritic fingers, imagine
a fresh place to start.

He may still read War & Peace
or drive the six hours to visit his brother
or perfect his barbequed ribs.
He might learn to use Twitter
or get high and play every one of his Dylan albums
in chronological order, listening to Blonde on Blonde twice.

But the light is waning. The maples are turning to scarlet
and caramel.

Winter advances.

He might paint her an apple that looks so real,
she'll fill her mouth with dry canvas.

LINDA DRACH is a poet, public health program analyst, and volunteer writing group facilitator for the nonprofit Write Around Portland. Her poetry has been published in *CALYX*, *The Write Launch*, *Clackamas Literary Review*, *The Timberline Review*, and elsewhere. In 2018, she was awarded a writing residency at PLAYA Summer Lake in Oregon's Outback. She is the current poet laureate of a small ranch house in Oregon, where she has an audience of one human and one exceptionally attentive pug.

AUDACIOUS

Joy McDowell

Before the speaker begins a PowerPoint presentation
on alligators in the Everglades, a friend leans in and whispers,
I've slept with five men in this room.
My lips are sealed with a nod and a weak smile.
All through gator snout pattern photos I wonder.

The teacher, probably. The marine scientist, I would bet.
The aging city maintenance worker—maybe a long time ago.
The alligator man. Oh, yeah. That, leaves one more. And the
screen lights up with boas, those nasty invaders dining on
vanishing swamp critters. I put my final chip on the veterinarian.

She shifts in her chair. Her wide-open brown eyes bathe
the speaker with seductive luster. He clicks his remote device
and a deer appears. Then come photos of snail kites, ibis, roseate spoonbill
and herons. The wood stork is silhouetted against a landscape of bladed grass.
The broad shoulder of the veterinarian cuts into view.

I tilt to see the screen. The speaker cannot abandon biology. Sexing alligators
presents challenges, he explains. Only smaller specimens can be held on
        their back
while a researcher examines their genitalia. She is gone before I have a chance
to invite her for a cup of coffee. I want the list. But she is off,
out in the dark parking lot hunting her next meal.

JOY MCDOWELL lives on Sky Mountain outside of Springfield, Oregon.
She writes story poems, short stories and traditional verse. Her alma
mater is the University of Oregon. She has a new kitten named Dorito,
a gift from one of her grandsons.

MEMBERS ONLY HONORABLE MENTIONS

AT HARRIET TUBMAN'S GRAVE IN FORT HILL CEMETERY, AUBURN, NEW YORK by Nancy Flynn: I admire the poet's economy of language, control of the line, and the subtle yet effective way that the strands of the poem are woven together. The use of rhyme also lends a musicality to the poem that is very pleasing. The ending of the poem, "One arrow shot into the Milky Way/at night, arrayed." in particular captured my attention and imagination.

THE DAY I DIE by Dale Champlin: I like the startling, sometimes surreal imagery in this poem especially the line comparing sex to "the kaleidoscopic push and pull." It's never easy to write about death (especially your own), but the poem presents new ways of thinking and coping with the inevitable. I admire the structure of the poem, three line stanzas staggered with italicized passages. There's also alliteration and other sound devices that enhance the poem. And the subject matter and the poet's use of the word "tulle" bring to mind Emily Dickinson. A very strong poem.

SLEEP WALKING IN THE JEWISH CEMETERY IN PRAGUE by VIVIENNE POPPERL: With its use of lines from Carolyn Forche's poem, dark imagery, and references to the Holocaust, the poem weaves a spell on the reader not unlike the paintings of Chagall which the poem describes. I liked the structure of the poem, the five quatrains, each one building on the next, and moving to the human contact in the penultimate stanza. The final stanza brings the reader face to face with the specter of a fate with no rescue in sight.

— *Michael Minassian*

NEW POETS

Judge Amy Miller

Amy Miller's *Astronauts* won the 2022 Chad Walsh Chapbook Prize from *Beloit Poetry Journal*, and her full-length poetry collection *The Trouble with New England Girls* won the 2017 Louis Award from Concrete Wolf Press. Her poems have appeared in *Barrow Street, Copper Nickel, Narrative, RHINO, Terrain, Tupelo Quarterly, Willow Springs*, and *ZYZZYVA*. She received a 2021 Oregon Literary Fellowship in Poetry and lives in Ashland, where she works for the Oregon Shakespeare Festival and is the poetry editor of the NPR listeners' guide Jefferson Journal. Website http://writers-island.blogspot.com Facebook: https://www.facebook.cm/amy.miller.3344913 IG: amymillerpoet Twitter:@amymillerpoet

Judge's Comments

The first-place winner, "Eyelashes in the Sink," is not afraid to go to the lengths it needs to in order to make the reader feel something. Poems about illness are tricky—so much has already been said—but this poem is an original take, its emotions unvarnished and very real, and the poet also chose this difficult villanelle form, against which this angry poem strains like a dog pulling on a leash. It's brilliantly rendered, true to the moment, and utterly memorable. The second-place winner, "Safe," is about as pared down as a poem can be; no words are wasted, and even the form is bare minimum—no capitalization, very little punctuation, except for those two delightful and surprising exclamation points. It goes to unexpected places, even though that box stays right where it is—which is the heart of the poem. "My Mother Said" took third place for its gentle motion—from the comment by the mother to glimpses of the teenager's life to the step forward in time in the fourth stanza, and then the earnest wish that the mother had been someone different. The poem never veers into sentimentality, and offers up one small surprise after the other as it whispers through this quiet story that resonates on so many levels.

I love the visual and grammatical fragmentation of the first honorable mention, "Ghosts"; its irregular stanza and line lengths bring to mind a torn fabric as it jumps from recollection to dream,

and then veers off in another direction at the end. I didn't know what
to expect from one line to the next—a wonderful thing in a poem.
"The apple tree is gone," the second honorable mention, looks as
well crafted visually as a stone wall, and reaches for the extra-
interesting words—"hale," "twining," and that amazing phrase,
"Left to new architects and / to gardens for animal desires." The
ambiguities—the relationship between the people, how much is
real and how much metaphor—heighten the pleasure of the poem.
And the third honorable mention, "Ordinary—A Ghazal," is joyful
and playful right from the first line, tossing around internal rhymes
and clever echoes at the ends of lines. It was a smart move to choose
"ordinary" as the recurring word, and this poet made the most of the
possibilities, celebrating language as the poem winds among humor,
dread, and everyday tenderness.

— *Amy Miller*

EYELASHES IN THE SINK
Christine Payne

Poison through your veins will flow
sickening all it grazes.
You're not here anymore, just go.

Brittle hair unwilling to grow
mocks in the shower drain.
Poison through your veins will flow.

An ambitious life now lying low.
A pariah, a ravaged phantom.
You're not here anymore, just go.

The delight of food a fading glow.
Old joys a torturous burden.
Poison through your veins will flow.

Sleep, deep sleep is all you know.
Better there than awake and aware.
You're not here anymore, just go.

Friends' platitudes are all for show.
Eyes betray their impatience.
Poison through your veins will flow.
You're not here anymore, just go.

CHRISTINE PAYNE is a cancer patient who is struggling with chemother-apy (the theme of her poem). She occasionally writes short stories but rarely poetry. She was having a bad day and this spewed out of her. She's not usually such a downer! Normally her free time as a retiree is spent playing Pickleball or walking her mini Australian Shepherds.

SAFE

Zachary Paul

whenever we move
i find

that crystal
bowl

unsolicited
wedding gift

exorbitant!
exquisite!
pristine

boxed
protected

safe

ZACHARY PAUL is a father, husband, schoolteacher, and poet.
Originally from a small coastal town in Oregon, he now resides
in the Willamette Valley.

My Mother Said

Ann Stinson

I'm glad he's kissing you there
instead of other places.

upon seeing the hickey
on my fifteen year old neck.

A neck normally bent
over a library book or
craned to see the river
from the top of a fir tree.

For years I told this story for laughs;
my cool, outspoken mother.

My fifty-nine year old self winces.
Wants to remember a soft shoulder touch,
maternal curiosity,

Do you like him?
Are you enjoying yourself?

Ann Stinson grew up on her family's tree farm on a ridge above the
Cowlitz River. After high school, she left rural life to study and work
in cities: Seattle, Tokyo, New York, and Portland. Her brother's
untimely death brought her back, to write about the land and its
people. She is the author of *The Ground at My Feet: Sustaining
a Family and a Forest*, published by Oregon State University Press
in November 2022. She joined OPA this year.

TRADITIONAL / THE GOLDEN SHOVEL

JUDGE James Benton

JAMES BENTON lives in La Grande, Oregon with his wife of 46 years, where he teaches English Writing at Eastern Oregon University. In prior lives he has worked as a sailor, an electrician, a bill collector, a musician, a night janitor, a retail clerk, and a private investigator. He earned his MA in creative writing at Cal State Sacramento and his MFA at Eastern Oregon University. Poetry, essays, reviews and memoir have appeared in *Word Riot, Convergence, Raintown Review, Tahoma Literary Review, Rattle,* and many others. His collections, *Sailor,* and *The Book of Sympathetic Magic,* are published by Winter Goose Publishing.

JUDGE'S COMMENTS

It was a pleasure to read the wonderful submissions for this contest, and it was difficult to select the winners from among so many clever entries. My main criteria were control of line endings and the relationship between the source text and the resulting poem on which it is based. Did the poet draw attention to the final word in each line, or did they craft sentences and line endings that softened the presence of language that is fixed in place by the form? Did the poet adapt the sense of the source text to fresh contexts adjacent to the source while avoiding mere duplication of meaning?

We never want to feel as though the line marches predictably or obviously to its conclusion, but instead hope the end of one line will carry us smoothly to the next. James Longenbach, in his book *The Art of the Line,* makes a distinction between line endings that align with syntactical units, which he calls parsed, and those that cut across syntactical units, which he calls annotated. Careful balance between parsed and annotated lines can produce surprising effects when lines are read in isolation. Sometimes a line is syntactically coherent when taken by itself, but when read in context with the following line, the syntax expands and offers multiple meanings.

Aside from control of line endings, the best poems in this form also absorb the borrowed words seamlessly so that they avoid drawing attention to themselves, while making a whole new poem separate from but akin to the sense of the source material.

Among the winners you will see a satisfying tension between Robinson Jeffers' hard monosylables and the fluid imagery of Dali's *Persistence of Time*, echoes of modernist word play and stream of consciousness, and sudden shifts of perspective that complicate otherwise pastoral scenes. These poems provide us with many surprises and represent the work of poets strongly in control of their craft. All the winners and honorable mentions are the work of fine poets, and I congratulate them all.

—*James Benton*

TRADITIONAL / THE GOLDEN SHOVEL
FIRST PLACE

OVER THE WINTRY

> *forest, winds howl in rage*
> *with no leaves to blow.*
> Soseki

Marvin Lurie

The trees are frost struck. Over
them like a cowl the
sky is gray and wintry.
A crust of snow covers the forest
floor. Everything bends away from the winds.
Wolves gather to howl
their dominion and mastery in
this cold world, where winds rage
through the trees, coating them with
ice. All small creatures hide. No
birds dare the branches. Only a memory of leaves
remains in some small hollows to
say there once was green, so harsh are the winds that blow.

MARVIN J. LURIE is a retired trade association executive who lives
in Portland, Oregon. He is an active member of the Portland poetry
community, including two terms on the Oregon Poetry Association
Board of Directors (OPA) and as a participant in several critique
groups. He is an almost perpetual poetry student at the Attic Institute
of Arts and Letters in Portland as a multi-year member of its Poets
Studio and a 2016-17 Fellow of its Atheneum.

TRADITIONAL / THE GOLDEN SHOVEL
SECOND PLACE

Our Eyebrows Raised Like Cathedral Arches
Linda Ferguson

> From a line in "A Carafe, that is a Blind Glass" by Gertrude Stein

Just what is a
Mrs. Malvarap, anyway? What kind
of trip or trap, chit or chat is that, clompity clap, in
lumberjack boots and sunflower hat, guzzling from a glass
with a striped bee sting bobbing among the absinthe ice cubes and
plaid and khakied dads? Perhaps a
proper relation (a cardigan of a cousin
or a niece pearled within a shell's clamped lips?) could explain a-
way our perplexity, although there's no spectacle
here – such a relief! – nothing a gabardine cop (and/
or a calico mother) couldn't iron with a pigeon coo pat, nothing
to stitch or staunch, despite a strange
flamingo she's flouncing up the street (not to church, though, A-
men to that)! Was there ever a Mister? Is there an eyelash in our pudding? A single
neon salmon? Was that her banana peel laugh taunting our stately steeple hurt?
Oh, knot your scarf, lest she season your boiled wool with some shocking color!

A five-time Pushcart nominee, LINDA FERGUSON is a writer of poetry, fiction and essays. Her chapbook *Of the Forest* was the 2nd place
winner of The Poetry Box Chapbook Prize 2021, and *Not Me: Poems
About Other Women*, is forthcoming from Finishing Line Press. Her first
chapbook, *Baila Conmigo*, was published by Dancing Girl Press. As a
writing teacher, she has a passion for helping students find their voice
and explore new territory. https://bylindaferguson.blogspot.com/

WITHOUT THE SOLACE OF GREEN
Tina Gaynon

After "Flights of Swans," Robinson Jeffers

Wear the persistence of memory, and
Live in the presence of melting watches
Grown cold and bound to a strap, the
Nightmare Dali kept alive so long:

Summer dawns, low tides on the coast.
Not one bird floats above the mountain
On the horizon. His clocks no longer vibrate.
The persistence of memory flows from

Paintbrush to canvas. Are these clocks bronze?
Able to resist the corrosive power of salt, to
Refuse to spark, to retard a patina of green.
Are the cases of these pocket watches bronze?

Their white faces with blue shadows fail to
Keep time. The shore offers no hint of green
Life. It insists on our irritable attention year
After year, tide after tide. It lives on after

The mind begins to wander, year after year,
Along bleak sands under cloudless skies, and
Finds it is never quite seven o'clock after all.

TRINA GAYNON'S poems appear in *Fire and Rain: Ecopoetry of California*, other anthologies, numerous journals, and a chapbook *An Alphabet of Romance* from Finishing Line Press. Her book *Quince, Rose, Grace of God* is forthcoming from Fernwood Press. She currently leads a group of poetry readers at the Senior Studies Institute in Portland and participates in the Ars Poetica community.

THEME / THE MOON

JUDGE A. Molotkov

A. MOLOTKOV is a supporter of Ukraine. His poetry collections are *The Catalog of Broken Things, Application of Shadows, Synonyms for Silence* and *Future Symptoms*. His memoir *A Broken Russia Inside Me* about growing up in the USSR and making a new life in America is forthcoming from Propitius. He co-edits *The Inflectionist Review*. His collection of ten short stories *Interventions of Blood* is part of *Hawaii Review* issue 91. Please visit him at https://amolotkov.com.

JUDGE'S COMMENTS

In "to keep them close" the speaker enters a pre-existing space now rendered inaccessible and deeply metaphysical: a universe of parents, whose life is extended and reflected through this investigation. "You" deploys surgically precise language and striking, evocative imagery in an injunction against the judgmental rightwing other. The poem sings love free of artificial constraints as it reminds the reader of our shared corporeality, and of our obligation to support others in living their lives unimpeded.

"You Can't Move Moonlight" is laconic and eerily effective in drawing the anxiety-inducing panorama of a hospital wing amid the greater world outside, a world into which the patient, lying on a narrow bed, projects their irresolvable longing.

"split ends" constructs a series of surreal, decentering images stitching together, in ways imagined rather than prescribed, the loose fabric of human existence. As in reality, in the poem our lives are comprised of fragmentary impressions that elude chronology and hover in the forefront of memory without aligning.

In "Sapphire Moon," the Earth's satellite performs the role of a mirror, allowing the speaker to study the reflection of their outer and inner realities, and to attempt synthesis and meaning-making.

"Photograph in Kyiv Post-2022" renders a nuanced, painful picture of a war-infected reality in a place whose peaceful citizens have been forcibly drawn out of their normal lives to participate in someone else's deadly farce.

— *A. Molotkov*

THEME / THE MOON FIRST PLACE

TO KEEP THEM CLOSE
Melanie Green

worry   all done now
for my mother   my father
their used-up old bodies
become smoke
weather
tidewater
become the before a beginning

gravel-throated autumn
brings wind
and the enormity
of leaving

many to love though
so here come worry
again
brother   friend   other friend

sickness travel round
what be the root of worry
but the want
to hold close

even so
some kind of ease
from the root
of here

bosc pears
porch talk
the up-dangled moon

i got   eyes   ears   tongue
heart wide as night   intimate
as bone
where the lost ones   loved
live

MELANIE GREEN's most recent collection of poetry, *A Long, Wide Stretch of Calm*, was published by The Poetry Box. Earlier books are: *continuing bridge* and *Determining Sky*. Her poems have been included in modern dance performances, and she was a participant in the 2000 Word & Hand collaborative arts exploration between poets and visual artists. She has been published in *Kosmos Quarterly*, *Buddhist Poetry Review*, *The Poeming Pigeon*, and elsewhere.

THEME / THE MOON SECOND PLACE

YOU
Robert Eastwood

who don't see a swing as metaphor
of your childhood, or a fly's behavior

as diagram of thought, & think about
pleasure as wrapper for sin—you, who block
throughways in towns deep in mid-America,
where, in mass, the righteous disguise their
fear of queerness—do you see that vaguely
colored, omnipresent moon? There are
some who yearn after love as different
as that moon—and you, who escape into
dreams of former ardor on solitary nights,
then, in the morning, get up with regret

on your palms—open a window—let sun
touch the honest baggage of your body.

ROBERT EASTWOOD is widely published. He has four books: *Snare*
(Broadstone Press, 2016), *Romer* (Etruscan Press, 2018). His third,
Locus/Loci, was published in 2019 (Main Street Rag). His fourth book,
Cantata Angeleno, was published by Broadstone Press May 1st, 2021.

YOU CAN'T MOVE MOONLIGHT
Susan Woods Morse

The moon is sickle shaped tonight.
It comes to you and lingers in the left square
of window pane just above your narrow bed.

How you long for something in the dark just beyond
that light! The hospital doors have opened to Spring,
their fluorescent bulbs blinking nonstop off - then on -
then off again like a mouth gaping, but you don't enter
their wide width.

You worry about their apparent invitation. You worry
that the moon is high, waxing, ringed round in a crown
of promises. If only you could hear the spring peepers
cheering it all on, if only you would take the needful
step beyond those cold, steely doors.

Outside the moonlight is so bright it drowns
any sounds coming from a myriad of dead mouths
and the constant whoosh of ventilators hovering.

SUSAN WOODS MORSE has a Masters degree in Literacy Education. She moved from Maine to Oregon in 2016. She served on the board of OPA and had her first chapbook, *In the Hush*, published by Finishing Line Press in 2019. Her work has appeared in journals such as *Cream City Review*, *The Mom Egg*, *Cirque*, *Willawaw Journal*, *Aji*, and *The Poeming Pigeon*. She won the NFSPS New York Poetry Forum Award in 2021.

30 AND UNDER

Judge   James R. Merrill

JAMES MERRILL taught high school English in California and at Chemawa Indian School in Salem—where he moved after earning his MFA at the Jack Kerouac School of Poetics, Naropa Institute in Boulder. After that, he taught Composition and Creative Writing at University of Colorado, Denver as well as one term as an exchange professor for CU - Denver in Beijing, China. After retiring from Chemawa, Jim has been busy teaching ESL to immigrants and refugees (including Ukraine) and Creative Writing at Chemeketa Community College in Salem.

Judge's Comments

"Smoke" contains searing father-son initiation pain with tender son-to-father reconciliation in real world imagery.

"Fetch" is a stealthy mixture of cute kitten rhymes with a second stanza that offers the juxtaposition of wild animal behavior that could come from inside that kitten.

"This Twilight" is at first a straight-ahead snapshot of the title, but with a nice example of blending senses, synesthesia: "song of tree crickets... becomes a feeling" and "fading heat becomes a sound."

— James R Merrill

SMOKE
TJ Foltz

Sometimes I peel my skin to see which parts hurt. Pull up scabs and ruin their healing; because you always thought I'd look better in scars and now, I hate to admit, so do I.

You'd balm your skin while passing the torch that burned you, left hand betraying the right; crackling of its molten anger only drowned out by the volume of the lessons between your words.

You taught me to measure my masculinity in empty liquor bottles and full prescriptions; your lesson that real men only dull their pain when they pretend it's for fun.

That service was inseparable from suffering, that goodness exists only to spite the dents in the same vessel and that as such it must be dented.

You taught of obedience through fear holding your doctrine to be as genuine as it is just; building paper walls for us to keep the world from the wood.

Your claim of course not to be mistaken, that you love me and that I am doomed. Yet fear was never a virtue, and your tradition cannot be my truth.

You taught that only love was set in stone; as if proof of rock's mortality was not sewn across the beaches or blown in the wind.

Perhaps I kicked drugs to become addicted to tattoos when they let me feel pain, and build to something that might be permanent, or because they make my scars look like something I could love.

You think I hate you, I wish I did. Pictures are so much more complicated than paintings, and conversations so much harder than poems. Burning your flag kept it off my shoulders, yet the memory of its embers brings more remorse than thrill.

...

And as such, I think of you whenever I smell smoke in my clothes. Nose filled with the rustic guilt of what I've done to keep myself warm. The loud blank memories that could fall anywhere between bonfires and funeral pyres.

TJ FOLTZ is an up and coming poet from here in Oregon who, like most poets, endeavors to find ways to communicate complex emotions through his poems. He's been writing consistently for two years and shows no sign of giving up his pursuit of his perfect poem.

FETCH

Julia Fritz-Endres

last week I trained Olive to fetch
a fuzzy blue ball, bring it back to me
with time, this little gray kitten learned not to claw
not to bite
I could only see her in the early morning and at night
so in the day she played
amid empty pizza boxes and
the dish rack and the moldy chili in the fridge
she ripped up string and draped pieces
like so many trophies on couch cushions
hung them from the arms of house plants
tucked them under the sink

the times when I waited for her to fall asleep
she spooned a teddy bear with gray fur like hers
and I imagined her waking to find her legs around it
this object that is almost a fellow being but with button eyes
I imagined her kicking its head clean off, back legs thumping
ripping out its insides
stretching its intestines across the floor
in a map for me to follow, to find my way back to her
then when I finally arrived
running up to the door before I could open it
refusing to eat until
I'd whispered her name.

JULIA FRITZ-ENDRES is an aspiring poet who spent much of her childhood curled up on a rock in the woods with a notebook in her lap. She has been writing poetry and short stories ever since. She grew up in Massachusetts, although has fallen in love with Portland, Oregon since moving there in 2021. She currently works in communications within the climate justice movement.

This Twilight

Christopher Foufos

These late summer evenings
are mystifying by nature.
As the days of August wane
and September nights bloom,
my senses seem to falter.
Textures and stimuli converge and blend
in this ethereal space
positioned between light and dark.
The song of the tree crickets
becomes a feeling.
The fading heat
becomes a sound.
I am in rapture
as I scrutinize the unique complexion
of each falling sun.
The colors bleed and pool
at the mountain clad horizon.
Hues of coral and mauve;
Seeping from the brilliant twilight.

CHRISTOPHER FOUFOS was born and raised in the small rural town
of Dundee, Oregon. He graduated from Portland State University
with an undergraduate degree in Social Science with an emphasis in
Anthropology and Indigenous Studies. His passions lie in writing
and travel, so he wishes to eventually graduate from his oh so romantic
position of moving boxes in a warehouse to a career in which he can
pursue something in those fields.

SPANISH LANGUAGE

JUDGE Amelia Diaz Ettinger

AMELIA DIAZ ETTINGER is a self-described 'Mexi-Rican,' born in Mexico but raised in Puerto Rico. As a BIPOC poet and writer, she has two full-length poetry books published: *Learning to Love a Western Sky* by Airlie Press, and a bilingual poetry book, *Speaking at a Time / Hablando a la Vez* by Red Bat Press, and a poetry chapbook, *Fossils in a Red Flag* by Finishing Line Press. Her poetry and short stories have appeared in literary journals and anthologies and have received honors and awards. A new full collection of poetry will be released by Red Bat Press in the fall. She has an MFA in creative writing from Eastern Oregon University. Presently, she and her partner reside in Summerville, Oregon with two dogs, two cats, and too many chickens.
https://ameliadiazettinger.pubsitepro.com/blog
https://www.facebook.com/ameliadiazettinger

LA LUNA DEL MEDIODÍA
Anna Jasinska

Al mediodía
camino insomne
bajo la luna brillante—

> rostro medio oculto, medio iluminado,
> colgado encima de las palmeras
> de Ocean Avenue.

Ambos deambulamos
pálido y fuera de lugar,
trastornados por el disco solar desnudo.

> En su cenit, arroja
> una niebla lúcida
> y los contornos nítidos se derriten.

Suenan cascabeles
bajo la sombrilla roja y blanca
de un carrito de helados.

> Al sonido de las campanas
> la gente, hasta ahora ajena e inconsciente,
> escucha y se levanta.

Como vestido con zapatos rojos,
ellos caen
en un desfile de baile delirante.

> Empiezan a marchar
> al ritmo solar y bailan un vals
> de distancia.

Una mascarada loca corre
por las calles,
al parque, a la playa

> cuanto más rápido, más alegre,
> y más profundo en un trance
> de carnaval.

Mientras, miro,
distante y curiosa,
bajo la luna del mediodía,

suspendida en algún lugar
entre el azul
y el cobalto.

SPANISH LANGUAGE FIRST PLACE

Midday Moon (English Translation)

Anna Jasinska

I walk sleepless
at midday
under the lustrous moon,

>   face half hidden, half lit,
>   hung overhead
>   of Ocean Avenue palms.

We both wander
pale and out of place, upset
by the naked solar disc.

>   At its zenith,
>   it casts a bright noontime mist
>   and crisp contours melt.

Jingle bells ring
under the red-and-white umbrella
of an ice-cream cart.

>   At the sound of the chimes,
>   a crowd, so far oblivious, listens
>   and rises.

Like dressed in red shoes,
they fall
into a delirious dance parade.

>   They start to march
>   to the solar tune and swing
>   in a distancing waltz.

An insane masquerade streams
through the streets,
to the park, to the beach—

>   the faster the cheerer
>   deeper and deeper
>   in a carnival trance.

While I watch,
distant and curious,
under the midday moon,

    suspended
    somewhere between azure
    and cobalt.

ANNA JASINSKA is a Polish-American poet and molecular geneticist specializing in the molecular basis of brain functions, behavior, and viral diseases. Her poems appeared or are forthcoming in the *California Quarterly*, *Cardinal Points*, *Oddball*, *Passengers Journal*, and *Cordite Poetry Review*.

DURAZNOS DE SANGRE INDIA

Jabez W. Churchill

Sé un poco de muchas cosas:
cuando podar y cuando sembrar,
cuanto tenta,
tarda en dar fruto
el durazno de sangre india.
Sólo sé lo que no debo hacer,
que flechas:
palabras dichas y no lanzadas,
actos cometidos y ometidos,
no importa sin voluntad,
a uno le dejan marca,
cicatriz encima del alma,
pozo negro en la de uno mismo.
El misterio mas insondable
todavía se me despliegue.
¿Cómo brota la afección?
y a pesar de escarchada, sequía y de plaga
¿Cómo florezca?
al fruto más raro,
más carnoso de todos
el amor.

CHEROKEE PEACHES (ENGLISH TRANSLATION)

Jabez W. Churchill

I know a little about a lot of things:
when to prune and when to sow,
how delicious-long it takes
for blood peaches to bear fruit.
I only know what not to do,
what arrows:
words said and left unspoken,
acts committed and of omission,
no matter unintended,
leave a mark,
a scar upon another's soul,
a sink hole in one's own.
The greatest mystery still unfolds,
how affection buds,
despite frost and drought and infestation,
how it blooms,
into the rarest,
most succulent of fruit,
love.

JABEZ W. CHURCHILL is the first bilingual poet laureate of Ukiah, CA, a poet teacher in California Poets in the Public Schools since 1998, and a member of the Ina Coolbrith Poetry Circle of Berkeley, CA for over 40 years.

FALL 2022 HONORABLE MENTIONS

POET'S CHOICE

1ST HONORABLE MENTION: "UPON LEARNING OF A FRIEND'S SUICIDE"
by Robert Eastwood

2ND HONORABLE MENTION: "AMELIA"
by Scottie Sterrett

3RD HONORABLE MENTION: "I'LL TELL YOU WHAT I SAW"
by Charles Castle

MEMBERS ONLY

1ST HONORABLE MENTION: "AT HARRIET TUBMAN'S GRAVE
IN FORT HILL CEMETERY, AUBURN, NEW YORK"
by Nancy Flynn

2ND HONORABLE MENTION: "THE DAY I DIE"
by Dale Champlin

3RD HONORABLE MENTION: "SLEEP WALKING IN THE JEWISH CEMETERY
IN PRAGUE"
by Vivienne Popperl

NEW POETS

1ST HONORABLE MENTION: "GHOSTS"
by Olivia Niland

2ND HONORABLE MENTION: "THE APPLE TREE IS GONE"
by M. Sean Stanley

3RD HONORABLE MENTION: "ORDINARY—A GHAZAL"
by Becky Chinn

TRADITIONAL / THE GOLDEN SHOVEL

1ST HONORABLE MENTION: "MIGRATION"
by Amelia Diaz Ettinger

2ND HONORABLE MENTION: "WITHOUT EFFORT"
by Brad Maxfield

3RD HONORABLE MENTION: "OF GWENDOLYN BROOKS"
by Barry Vitcov

THEME / THE MOON
1st Honorable Mention: "split ends"
   by Daniela Elza
2nd Honorable Mention: "Sapphire Moon"
   by Judson Hyatt
3rd Honorable Mention: "Photograph in Kyiv Post-2022"
   by Carey Taylor

30 AND UNDER
1st Honorable Mention: "Racing"
   by Olivia Niland
2nd Honorable Mention: "To The Cabbage White Butterfly
   Who Frequents My Lettuce Patch"
   by Caroline Holm
3rd Honorable Mention: "Earth"
   by Levi Krum

SPANISH LANGUAGE
No Honorable Mentions in This Category